Book Ends

by Rodney Bowsher

Dedication

To the late John Skinner, a lifelong friend of many talents.

He made me laugh and introduced me to the work of Philip Larkin.

Acknowledgements

The Author is grateful to:

Heather Chadwick: for editorial and technical guidance

Philip G. Keen: for his cover artwork (pkeen30@btinternet.com)

Lorraine Bowsher: for additional editorial support

Mark C. Skinner: for layout & editing (mark@bytescomputers.co.uk)

The late Philip Larkin: for his letter of encouragement

Contents

Long ago

Long ago,
Underfoot and in the way,
The rubber ball of me
Bounced about the kitchen
Into my mother's bell-like apron
As she house-worked through the day.

Her apron smelt of recent endeavours:
Lavender polish, cake-mix and Bisto.
Together, we listened to 'Music While You Work'.
I bounced as she worked
And we sang and we sang and we sang.
Long ago.

Anybody's Mother

As we knelt
Before the 'in-house' holy talker
Officiating
From his temporary, pack-away altar,
It became uncomfortably clear
That his left-trouser leg
Was definitely shorter.
More than that:
His socks did not match -
One grey and one black.
He seemed tired, indifferent,
As if he'd 'done too many' that morning.
And he got her surname wrong!
It devalued the occasion
From the spiritual to the mechanical.

It confirmed
That yours, mine, anybody's mother,
Is such a monumental figure
That seeing what's left,
Brought from the chapel of rest,
Reduces so much endurance
To mere dust;
Scooped out in handfuls
From a returnable urn;
Then blown back again
To the town from which she came:
A faint cloud of powder
Caught by a gust.

It seems so wrong . . .
So unjust !

Nothing Happens Now I'm Old

Nothing happens now I'm old
But when I was a kid I remember . . .
A war-time cafeteria, the 'People's Pantry',
Crumbly and derelict,
The result, my mother said, of a direct hit
From a bomb that dropped at lunch-time,
Killing over eighty people
Cruelly deprived of
Their suet pud and treacle.

Nothing happens now I'm old
But when I was a kid I remember . . .
Trying to learn to cycle
On the path at the side of our house,
Which was too short to learn on
And too hard to fall on
Without bashing up the bike
Which belonged to my sister
For going to a factory
Which she didn't like,
But which helped her save
For my new, birthday bike.

Nothing happens now I'm old
But when I was a kid I remember . . .
The man across the alley
Kept chickens in a creosoted hutch.
And when they went to the toilet,
Real eggs came out of their crutch.
I thought this was magic
But mum said he was tight,
'Cos he kept all the eggs.
So I lit a banger on bonfire night
And chucked it at the chickens,
Who went mad with fright.
Then upon the toilet,
They were quite all right.

Nothing happens now I'm old
But when I was a kid I remember . . .
Old rags for goldfish and the muffin man
And my mother's orange ration-book
With which I ran to the shop that sold everything,
From coal to candles and salt in lumps
And little gas-mantles
Which you may have seen
If you've ever been in a caravan.

Nothing happens now I'm old
But when I was a kid I remember . . .
Being taken to London, by my sisters to the Sales
And making them cross by always getting lost
And trying to stamp on pigeons' tails.
I remember the way it was dark at mid-day
And a policeman saying that the Queen was away
And Percy Dalton's chestnuts and London Zoo
And my sisters saying, "We are *not* with you!"
And always wiping my ice-creamy face
And saying I was old enough to tie my own lace.
And although the train going home had talking wheels
And the engine had a cold and sneezed out steam;
What made me happier than all I'd seen,
Was the way Mum smiled at my jumping-bean.

Nothing happens now I'm old
But when I was a kid I remember . . .
Bashing my head against a classroom radiator,
Whilst stooping on the ground for a penny
And then blackness and visions
Of jars and provisions in my favourite sweet shop,
Until one by one, the jars went away
And all that remained was a bright little dot
Which I prayed would stay and I've never forgot
That my little boy's reason for not letting go
Was my little boy's dot, which meant I'm here
So no giving up. And because I tried,
I never died; I never died.

Nothing happens now I'm old
But when I was a kid I remember . . .

For Students of Psychology

Hot, summer's day.
Bend in the road.
Sulky-faced boy,
Sat on the kerb,
Hurling a rock
At a Labrador dog.

Dog keeps bringing it back,
Even when it hurts.
Bringing it back; bringing it back !
Boy hugs dog
And bursts into tears,
Bestowing on the dog
Pat, after pat, after pat.

Now then. . .
What do you make of that !?

Saddle Joint

It took many weeks to complete:
My lovingly-crafted firescreen,
With its oiled finish and saddle-jointed feet.
Also learned: the handling, purpose and sharpening of tools
Like 'setting the bevel' on a chisel tip,
Then sharpening it with an oil stone, snugly tucked up
Inside a hardwood case, and - best of all -
Wiping it clean with cotton waste.

We learned the recipe for fish-glue,
Learning too, 'best-practice' rules
Like measure, check and measure again
And the repeated mantra :
Always cut *inside* the line !
Our instructor's other refrain?
'Remember lads, you can always take it off
But you can *never* put it back again.'

Finally, one sunny afternoon,
Mum's present was ready.
Perched on the bars
Of my sister's big bike,
I launched myself
Across the busy A4.
The low sun dazzled me.
A lorry loomed; I back-pedalled furiously.
My screen slid over the bars,
Missing the lorry and several cars,
Before coming to rest in three pieces.

Stunned, I collected the bits –
Unlikely now to fit.
So much for saddle joints!
At home, to soothe me, Mum tried in vain,
Again and again,
To stand it in the fireplace, but it refused –
Feet and legs remaining stubbornly apart,
Broken, like my heart but wait!
A redeeming thought has suddenly occurred:
A *wooden* fire-screen ? How absurd !
. . . I should have chosen metal work.

The Eleven Plus

The playground didn't need a fence
To distinguish the grammar boys
From us secondary-moderns.

They had uniforms;
We didn't.
They played pocket-chess;
We played marbles.

They enjoyed a science lab
With Bunsen burners
Whereas we 'practical' learners
Settled for woodwork.

At concerts
They had 'real' instruments;
Violins and clarinets:
They could read music.

We had a skiffle group;
Tea chest string basses,
Wash boards, kazoos
And blank, mutant faces.

They had mothers and fathers;
We had mums and dads.
They had masters;
We had teachers.

But for all we never had
We'll still end up the same …
Under the crust, them and us,
With or without, the eleven plus.

Hospital

Flashing lights and sirens remind the unwell
That this must be the place:
The location at the top of their letter.
This sprawling Legoland of tower-blocks, annexes,
Research labs. and clinics of every discipline,
Seamlessly plugged together - the old and new -
Prosthetically joined; this high-rise waiting factory:
Our local hospital.

Inside, flags of signage bristling with arrows,
Punctuate the routes down mirror-polished corridors
Where the old, the young and in-betweenies
Dance the 'you go first' hornpipe
To the accompaniment of opening-closing, hissing lifts.

Hunched-over aged with saw-dusty heads
Wave sticks like mine detectors
As they sway along,
Determined to be punctual,
Even if it means not being seen
In their order of arrival.

Advancing more cautiously,
The sounds and sights of
The squeaky-wheeled 'motorised' brigade
Rattle past with their stainless gallows,
Sporting bags of plasma hanging from the gibbets,
Swinging and twisting,
Umbilically attached to their drivers -
All of whom sport the jewellery of their needs:
Canalures and I.D. bracelets
Around bruised rainbow-coloured wrists.

Overtaking them all, the dodgers and bluffers,
The self-appointed shop stewards
In thick gowns and racing slippers,
Moving quickly along the 'rat runs'
Like battery-powered tea cosies
Determined to reach the 'forbidden zones'
Of shop and fire door, where relief awaits
From a hurried, wet roll-up.
Pockets bulging, they slink back to the wards,
Poker-faced, with frowned-upon cargoes,
Their antidotes to boredom and 'do you good' dinners.

'Pop and prattle' magazines, chocolate bars, crisps, popcorn
And – top of the bad-boy list – especially for diabetics,
A suicidal bottle of Lucozade, all of which is smuggled back
To be discreetly stashed in bed-land.

Distracted by pagers, doctors 'sorry, sorry' along busy corridors.
Weighed down with files, their black, spidery stethoscopes
Clinging to their necks as they bump into new arrivals,
Similarly distracted, by worrying appointments with
Same; in whose gift it will be
To reveal good or bad news.

Round the back, 'Goods Inwards' bays
Open up to check the manifests of lorries,
Pneumatically lowering tall, wire cages,
Stacked with towels and bed-linen.
While around the front, adapted people-carriers do the same,
Lowering the disabled and wheel-chair bound.

Throughout the day, traffic, vehicular and human,
Approaches and departs:
Mini-cabs, medical supplies, ambulances, 'park and ride' buses,
Out-patients, visitors, wheel-chair and crutch users,
The latter, helped by sons and daughters,
Donating a hand or forearm to support unsteady elders.

The day wears on.
A helicopter clatters off from the roof,
Quickly replaced by wheeling, squealing seagulls
And cooing feral pigeons flapping up to gutters
With scavenged bits of Eccles cake and bread crust;
An aviator's supper.

Day-shift nurses – cardigans over uniforms –
Search for keys as they cross to the car-park,
Where dusk has signalled the freeing-up of spaces.
It is clouding over, light is fading, temperatures dropping.
The buzz of traffic comes to rest.
By now the car-park
Just couldn't care less.

In the wards, the night-shift start their checks:
Pills dispensed, blood pressures and temperatures taken,
Resting on chests, paperbacks are sleepily read;
Often, the same page twice, before slipping to the floor.
Abandoned T.V. sets flicker,
Overhead lights dim
And bed-bound captives, mixing yawn with sigh,
Tune-up for their nightly symphony of coughing and snoring
Accompanied by the nocturnal cry of the anxious and frightened:
'Nurse! Nurse!'

As night closes in, the stuffiness thins.
A welcome breeze fidgets with the curtains.
And for those with one leg in and one leg out, the tension eases.
Now, with blessed relief, the hospital exhales and finally, finally . . .
Sleeps.

December 14th

At seven am, I phoned:
"Have you got a bed?"
"Yes. Come on in!" they said.
My wife had a cold
So - no kiss -
Just a No.3ish cuddle, instead.
My dog, being insecure,
Having seen my bag by the door,
Ate what he'd deposited on the kitchen floor,
Then leapt up to kiss me.
Fortunately, he missed me.
He too, got a No.3
But at arm's length and quickly.

The first nurse I had to see,
Was a retirement returnee
Who said, laughing nervously,
"You know more than me!
I just can't get this canalure in!"
She sent for a 'boy' doctor;
Tall and thin, with designer-stubble on his chin.
He tried, and failed three times.
By now, there was blood on the bed.
"It's cool! I'll send for someone
Who knows what they're doing," he said.
My confidence ebbed!

In the event,
The surgeon came down
In his rubberized gown.
"What! No canalure?
No bloods. No E.C.G. done?
An hour has passed
Since I should have begun!
Give me that pink one -
The 'extra-thin'.
There you go; job done!
Now. Get him in. Get him in.
Get him IN!"

In the theatre
They covered me with leads,
Then clamped my arms.
Like Gulliver!
"Are you ready, Mr.B?"
"No!
Can someone scratch my eyebrow
And the end of my nose?
Can I have a bottle?
I need a pee!"
"O.K. Sir, off we go . . .
You'll feel sleepy soon:
Just go with the flow."

Beyond the humming
And hydraulic smells
His disembodied voice:
"You're doing *very* well!"
Jargon was exchanged
Which I couldn't understand.
Oh, for the comfort of a nurse's hand...
Twice the mask for the oxygen slipped,
Diverting air above my lip,
Till finally, someone noticed
And altered it.

Next, came the invasive part:
Under the collar-bone, make a breach.
Find two veins, which reach the heart.
Thread a wire into each
And 'slot the engine' into the car.
German, of course, the best, by far!
A powder-compact 1cm thick
Called, I think, a Biotronik;
A terminal on top,
For wires to fit.
Its medical name,
Implantable Cardioverter Defibrillator.
To you and me – an I.C.D.
So; what's it do, this palm-sized pack?
When the heart reveals an arrhythmic attack,
The machine responds and shocks it back -
To a regular pulse.

For it to fit requires a three inch slit,
Into which, from powerful thumbs,
Real pressure comes as he presses down,
Deep into my chest,
Until the foreign, foreign object
Comes to rest where it will function best.

Its wires connected,
For the next five years, that is that,
Until they open me again
When the battery goes flat.

I thought health - like education or justice -
Was something you got more or less of
According to your means.
I was wrong, it seems:
For a pensioner,
Thirty thousand quid on the N.H.S.
Must be the ultimate gift -
A life snatched back
On December 14th.
All in all, a remarkable day,
Wouldn't you say?

Waiting Room

In the field
A fox flashes its tail
And trots on by.

Up above
Head and eye,
A jet parts the sky.

Outside
A scaffolder's lorry
Rattles past.

In my bed
I murmur and turn over,
Pulling up the cover;

Waiting and wondering,
Is it time yet,
To die?

Charlie from Connecticut

As daylight fades,
As hail-stones plop,
As buzzard flaps off
From rainswept rock,

As weakened resolve
Embodies the fear
That a *'goddamned box canyon*
Is what we got here!',

Charlie from Connecticut
Comes to a stop,
Between the impulse at the bottom
And his snap-shots at the top:

Lost, on a donkey
On the first day of his holiday,
Halfway up a mountainside
In Greece.

In a Motel Opposite Disneyland

As I lie here on my Disneybed,
Picking out the Disneys
From between my Disneybread,
All over Disneytown
The Disneylights are going down.
And when the Disneypeople
Have put out their Disneycats,
Turned off all their oil wells
And locked their Cadillacs,
Unlike the visitors - hicks and farmers -
Disneytown will kneel
In its Mickey Mouse pyjamas
To say. . .

' God bless America and keep me Disneysafe.
Put Disneys in my charge-account,
Put Disneys on my plate.
Despatch my Disneywife back to my Mother in Disneylaw
And grant me, Lord, much more, more, MORE !
Send me Disneydames and stop my hair from turning grey.
Disney me to Washington, before it's washed away!
But right now, thank you for the Disneybounteous way,
You sent so many suckers into town today.'

If ever you are there lying on a Disneybed,
Don't touch the Disneys or the Disneybread.
When night-time comes, I'd recommend instead,
That you peel off the sticker under Minnie Mouse's knicker
And pour yourself a shot of best Walt Liquor.
Amen, Amen, Amen.

Butterfingers

Self-motivation
I long for it constantly,
Always letting go, resignedly.
What chance of a mortgage
For a softy like me ?

Oh, to be back in the Army;
Life was effortless then.
Someone would have screamed,
"I want you all outside at ten –
To learn the 'Taking Out of Mortgages!'"

Sentry Duty

Around the backs of N.A.A. F. I.'s
At four in the morning,
Between last night's empties
And khaki washing,
Older soldiers squat
Behind piles of coke
To ease their stint
With a crafty smoke
In front of warm, sooty boilers.

Each man is issued
(In case of trouble)
With a gymnast's club,
A torch and a whistle
Which they must blow
(Three blasts),
If terrorists show
To rob the armoury.

That, should it happen,
Is when older soldiers run,
Before an officer comes:
A pink-faced subaltern,
Armed with five O-levels,
A hyphenated name
And a pet yellow Labrador.

Photographic Memory

Speaking as one
Of the hitch-hiking soldiery
Who vied for lifts
Between London and Camberley,
Two - who stopped -
Remain
Locked in the memory.

One, in a van,
For buttering bread with one hand,
As we spread past Windsor
At fifty miles an hour.

And the other, for a photo
No bigger than a halfpenny,
Of his beautiful wife and children,
Which he'd stuck over the 70.

The Queen's Own Expendables

The Tali' bullet,
Fired from a dried river bed,
Struck young Private Anyone -
Of the Queen's Expendables -
On the finished side of his half-barbered head
As he perched on an ammo box, in shorts and flip-flops,
A white bed sheet around his bare shoulders,
While his mate, Jim, gave him a cooling trim
The sheet changed from white to red as he dropped,
Like his cigarette - onto the Afghan sand,
The loss of this 'asset' was recorded at 1630 hours -
Kabul time.

In London, simultaneously, at 2100 hours, GMT.
In the 'Private Members' bar,
The lad's home-town MP sipped his G&T,
Stroked his secretary's knee, fed her a canapé
And dragged her impatiently into the night -
Not knowing or caring
That another 'own goal' had been added to the score
Of a soldier's fight in a politician's war.

The Glass Divide

There are two sides of a plate glass divide,
On one of which, our nature resides.
You may suit the 'feisty' side, which says,
'When life gets tough and you need a hand,
There's one on the end of your wrist.'

Perhaps you'd be happier on the softer side?
Following a leader.
Taking orders, not giving them?
Saying yes to less.
Caring and sharing, not grabbing and having.

Remember,
Whatever you do,
The glass is a construct of our nature,
Meant not for climbing over…
Just looking through.

In The Cold

It's cold here in the churchyard
Where the pigeons peck
And the girl throws bread
In good-natured defiance
Of the 'No Feeding' sign.
Her in *her* seat; me, in mine.

I should have worn a coat, perhaps,
Or not have come at all
For the good such places do;
Accenting her in her defiance,
Me in my suit,
Her in her duffel-coat,

Me in my lunch-break,
Her in her twenties
And me in my thirties,
In the Autumn,
In the churchyard,
In the cold.

The Church

Even for the irreligious who cannot pray,
Or know what to believe or say -
Surely the Church can loosen the knot
Which separates those who come
From those who do not.
Gothic arches, mossy steeples,
Towers, stone-works, everything,
Including praying hands, points upwards
From where the 'chairman'
Allegedly looks down upon us.

The Church needs us to pay as well as pray;
So there are fetes, bazaars, jumble sales
And bobbing apples in splashy pails.
'Send a Cow To Africa' a leaflet urges.
Funds also come from christenings,
Weddings and funerals.

Vicars, male and female, tilt forwards and backwards,
Like white paper bells, dispensing wafers and wine,
Saving handshakes till the end of the service.
Inside the door, at the blunt end,
Squats a huge, stone bird-bath, for christening.
At the pointed end, knuckles gripping the pulpit rail,
The vicar looks out to sea, like a passenger,
Leaning out from the promenade deck.
Meanwhile, aged question marks weave up and down,
Working the pews with upholstered offertory bags,
Hoping for the chink of coin drop.

On Sundays, singing echoes
Around cold, stone columns and bum-polished pews,
Sometimes in and sometimes out of tune.
Increasingly, the clergy are 'New Age,'
Strumming guitars or squeezing accordions,
Competing with the dragon's breath of the organ.
The line-up of the choir resembles a row
Of Russian dolls: baritones, tenors,
Contraltos and sopranos - their chubby cheeks
Ballooning out above sharply-pleated ruffles,
Plum puddings on a plate.

In summer the church becomes a venue
For Arts and Craft shows:
Seascapes, landscapes, portraits,
Embroidered dog and cat cushions,
(Which never include your own pet's breed),
Pottery, (including flower pots you mustn't add water to)
And smaller items (but never egg cups).

Through an open side door, giant kettles
Bubble and steam, sending tempting smoke signals
To the peckish and thirsty from the tea room:
Scrumptious trays of lemon drizzle cake,
Mixed fruit slices and iced bun rounds beckon.
For the thirsty, 'builders', herbal tea, cordials and
Spring water are eagerly quaffed.
"Thank you, Sir. Thank you, Madam.
Choose a table and we'll bring it over."

Outside the main door, a parked mobility scooter
Reveals its owners faith by the scarf and programme
Left openly in the front basket.
Approaching the door, a determined lady
Persuades a wilful spaniel to 'sit'
On a convenient gravestone before going inside.
Departing cars bump down from half-on,
Half-off perches on the nearby pavement,
Before trying to turn in the narrow road.

Then it's time for home: time to kick off shoes;
Tear away tissues from cruets, tea-sets,
Artwork and embroidered throws,
The possession of which leaves owners
Half suspecting that one day they may return
To the permanent embrace of this ageless monument,
With its green beds, its names and dates
Above their heads…its arms forever round them.

Best Friend

Before his journey into eternity,
One I knew personally has been put on show;
Resting on rollers, in a wooden lozenge,
Model number - such and such,
Design style - so and so.

Without camping on doorsteps,
Fifty years of friendship
Has reached an end, so on a seat
Within reach of my lifelong friend,
I fill in from memory
What the speaker leaves out:

His time in the 'Paras'.,
Jumping from 'Hastings' and 'Beverleys',
The outrageously *camp,* yellow Renault
Which he drove through a general's parade;
His tours of duty, in the heat of Bahrain
Or the cold of Belfast, warding off rain.

His skills as a jazz trumpeter
And 'big band' orchestrator;
His role as Headmaster and school Governor;
His love of poetry and Larkin:

The funniest, wisest man I knew,
Always searching for what was true.
If he could see himself now, I know what he'd do…
Bang on the lid and shout,
"So what's it like in there then: What's it all about !?"

But I'll let it go…
Because in death as in life,
Those who know,
Never show.

The Dishonourable Member

Be in no doubt,
I sit firmly on the fence,
Ruling nothing in
And nothing out,
Which helps me keep my seat
And explains why -
When l cry -
The tears from my right eye
Roll down my left cheek.

God.con

When I got to heaven
What was God's greeting;
'Can't stop now...
Going to a meeting.'

Death's Fashion Show - 1975

Seven miles West
Out of Key Biscayne in Florida,
At sixteen knots and sixteen years of age,
Amanda McArthur
In her father's cabin-cruiser,
Wrenches out the stop-cock
And sinks beneath the waves;
Becoming no more dead in death
Than when alive.

"And now! For those sunny days at sea, ladies! Amanda's bandana comes
in red, white or blue and is in double-sided silk by Balmain. Her bolero-
jacket and trousers are in brush-denim with white saddle stitching, availa-
ble in all colours and the rope-soled canvas deck shoes are optional. Thank
you, Amanda. Thank you!"

In a high-rise apartment
Off the Avenue Louise,
With her husband at his girl-friend's
And her neck back on a stool,
A quiet Brussels housewife
Drinks a can of caustic-soda
And screams as she burns
For her children in school;
Becoming no more dead in death
Than when alive

"Next, ladies! For something smart, yet practical to wear around the
home: Isabelle is modelling a hopsack skirt, which is cut on the bias, with
the hem below the knee. This comes in camel or black, and the roll-neck
sweater can be worn outside the waist band or tucked in as shown with a
simple, little belt. To add something special to its classical simplicity the
sweater is threaded with lurex and - in keeping with the autumn - comes in
copper, mead or sepia.. To complete the ensemble, the little buckled shoes
are by Jourdan of Paris, in black, tan or navy and the buckles are detacha-
ble. Doesn't she look elegant? Thank you, Isabelle. Thank you!"

With a photo of his wife
Placed at the back of the oven
To remind him of the reason
Why his head is at the front,
Deserted Thomas Jaimeson
Of Cornwall Gardens, Kensington,
Slips off into oblivion –
Discoloured and defunct;
Becoming no more dead in death
Than when alive.

"And so, to finish our show, here is something for the gentlemen. Thomas is wearing the latest line in lounge-suits: made of a wool and mohair mixture, with a chalk-stripe running through, this comes in brown, black or navy, in a twelve-ounce cloth. The jacket has double-vents at the back and is elegantly waisted with clover-leaf lapels. The shirt is in silk with a buttoned fly-front. The shoes are made by Churches and they also come in brown. The tie is Yves St. Laurent from a range of eighteen colours and we thank you all sincerely for your warm applause tonight. Incidentally,Thomas, we thank you too! Now, when everyone is ready, there are cocktails in the lobby and things on sticks as well. Thank you once again for supporting our show. Bye now everybody. Bye now, everyone!"

"Charlie! Bert! Quick word, lads . . . Nice job today. Sorry about the short notice: Look, can I pencil you in for the Caxton Hall next Wednesday? Same old crap: Box-section catwalk, silver sides, black top, mini-turnaround on the end, gold tables and chairs, table-lighters. Waiters 'll do the drinks and nibbles. Right! I'll let you get on wiv' packin' up. Word of warnin' though! Watch out for the old bird in charge. You can't miss 'er: Skinny, funny glasses, clown's tights, flits about like a sparrow in a bird-barf. If she says anyfink about 'elpin 'em wiv' their coats or showin' 'em 'aht, ignore 'er and take my advice: before they go, check the champagne-flutes and the table-lighters, 'cos you just don't know. Not wiv' buggers like these ! Next Wednesday then: Caxton Hall, seven am. sharp! They want a sponsor's banner across the main entrance: VAGUE MAGA-ZINE WELCOMES YOU ! Somefink like that. Anyway... The Caxton's always a nice little earner and - as they say - the show must go on - the show must go on...!"

Out the Back

I was visiting an old friend
At a new address.
"Mind if l look out the back?"
I ventured to suggest.

To the left and right
Between fenced-off rungs,
I saw top halves of mums
Among geraniums
Whilst ahead, beyond his shed,
The allotments:

Smoke smudging up
Into a brilliant blue sky,
Fired by gone-over clover
And rhubarb shard;
Bottle-tops on strings
Frustrating predatory wings
From robbing bean-stalks
Fit for Jack.

Above the fire's crackle,
The conspiratorial cackle
Of two weathered old heads -
Steeped in a life-time of veg
Could be faintly heard:
Criticising composts,
Complimenting carrots
And relishing the rot
On a rival's radishes.

Old coots,
Nurturing young shoots.
Old horticultural mates
Comparing rakes.
Well . . . good luck
And God bless 'em –
Loamy old loons . . .
Be burnt themselves soon –
Done by men with black ties
From the Co-op.

Book Ends

Two book ends:
Birth and death,
In the grip of which,
Wedged in tight
…Is *life*
And the task of
Savouring and saving it.

Pressing ever closer,
The right-hand end
Is terminal
And the one to watch,
Whereas the left-hand end -
Which started the deceit -
Patiently waits,
Until both ends meet.

Man with a Tin

Stood inside the door
He's the first one you see
Every second Thursday
At the Poetry.

He collects our fee
In an antique tin, donates a grin
Then lets us in to jostle for seats
Amongst the bric-a-brac.

His name doesn't matter,
Nor his age;
Only that he likes my work
And thinks I do 'good rage!'

He monitors not just money
But the comings and goings
Of 'people things';
A thankless chore –

Which he has in common
With millions more
Who volunteer to be batteries
For the torch bulbs of others.

Just a man in a doorway
Holding a tin,
Seldom seen or heard
Except to let us in,
That we might further the cause
Of the spoken word.

Moving Day at the Manor

"Your ladyship,
It might sound very petty,
But my men and I agree -
Having checked the inventory,
There's still an item missing -
A cup of bleedin' tea!"

On Achieving Distance with the Driver

When you hit the ball,
Forget about 'position'.
Just pretend
It's a politician.

Pensioner's Lament

" Sorry, old chum !
But this I know . . .
So slow and fickle
Does wisdom flow,
Into buoyant flood
From naïve little trickle,
That just when we know . . .
It's time to go !"

Bentleying Over Backwards

"Do hurry up! For goodness sake!
The Bentley is on a line!"
Whinnied the posh lady,
In the posh shop,
To the awkward, young man
Who was thinking at the time,
About rent; rates; the hole in his shoe
And the bricks in his heart
Which a lonely life threw.

"I'll metch the fanager . . .
I mean, I'll . . ."
Awkwardly stuttered
The awkward young man
But, being the manager himself,
He fetched instead,
His most senior-looking junior -
Who had as many shoes and girls
As he had smiles and knew -
Unlike the manager -
That he was tactfully being groomed
For the poor sap's job.

"My word! Madam is looking fetching!"
Said the fetched, young dude.
"I'd have come myself -
If I'd known it was you.
An' I'm sorry Madame 'as 'ad this t'do,
But between your lovely face and mine . . .
He's new!"

Rescue Mission

Shake, shake, shake the tin
And look in: three left.
Bang it on the side
Of the saucepan's rim;
Bang, bang , bang !
And look in: two left.

Shake, shake, shake the tin
And look in: one left.
Perhaps a wristier action,
A flick and a spin
To work the contents up to the rim?
Look in: *Still* one left.

Scrape, scrape, scrape!
Is a wooden spoon the thing?
Nope; too fat.
I need something thin.
Shall I just give in
And throw what's left into the bin?
Got it! A metal spoon;
I know where they're kept.
Now: scrape, scrape, scrape!
And look in.
ONLY ONE BEAN LEFT!

Out it comes then,
The last one in the can,
Rejoining its mates
In the unlit pan.
So . . . why keep doing it,
Rescuing beans?
Is it compulsive tidying?
Is it thrift; is it greed?
Or something left behind
Which reminds me of myself?
Gathering dust on a pantry shelf,
Bored from being stored.
If so, then dust me!
Someone, *please*
Come and dust me!

If Only He'd Have Said

Stooped and breathless, he hobbled into the kitchen;
Pains in his head, his chest and his feet.
He tried to talk but she said,
"Sorry. Time for the show. Must go, or I won't get a seat!"
When she left he went back to bed.
When she came home, he was dead.

She found, networking around with like-minded friends,
That for simple tasks, husbands could be useful.
They could offer financial support; drive on motorways;
Mend stuff; take rubbish to the tip and saw things in half.
They were handy and - like elastic bands -
Could be used again and again if stretched to the limit.

This just wasn't fair: *So* inconsiderate!
She sipped a glass of port and thought and thought…
What she needed now was a disclaimer - an alibi
For the years of widowhood ahead.
She settled for a phrase, locked in many a widow's head…

' If *only* he'd have *said* !'

A Widow's Thoughts

My husband's remains are on a hill,
Scattered against a tree.
Back here in the house in a stainless tin,
The remains of a loaf,
Shared by him and me.

The last slice was his -
I always left a slope -
But the end of this loaf
Shows a perfect cut
Of precisely ninety degrees.

I feel him watching, over my shoulder,
So I must try harder,
Slice straighter
And show how I've learned
To cut and to cope.

Dawn Chorus

From my bed
I woke and looked up
To see a goal post of light
Around the window blind.

I heard the herd
In the fields beyond...
'Moo-moo, moo-moo...'
On and on and on.

The owl added *its* little song,
'Too-wit, too-woo, too-wit, too-woo.'
Next, a different din
As the pigeons joined in,
'Coo-coo, coo-coo, coo-coo.'

Sleep was prized away
As a fly came to stay,
'Buzz-buzz, huzza-huzz.'

I could just see,
The little hand on the five
And the big hand on the three.

The answer - it seemed to me,
Was a nice cup of tea.
But I dropped off again -
So it wasn't to be.

Destiny

Destiny? Oh yes, we all have one of those.
For some, it ends in awkwardness;
Old bones and habits;
Unfulfilled dreams;
And in 'did' exposed as 'didn't'
By the sneer of another year.

So that as deeds recede
And resolve concedes
To the yawn between sofa and solution,
Old bodies in new days,
Coughing for effect,
Search with less and less conviction
In the pigeon-holes of conscience,
But let artful tongues excuse themselves
Through alibis of age
For a life of chances lost
And our destinies revealing
We are less the sum of our dreams
Than the sum of our physical needs . . .

An arm-chair;
A fire;
The racing page;
A mug of tea;
A biscuit to dip;
A dog;
Slippers
And a cardigan with pockets.

Then What, for a Laugh?

Firstly, the motorway:
Smooth and fast.
Secondly, a side-road:
Gravelled and coarse.
Then through a gateway:
'Please Shut After Use'.
So to the river
And the boat
At last.
Cast off for'ard!
Cast off aft'!

Oh! Lovely chug
And petroleumed pop!
Oh! Varnished cabin
With lamp on top.
Oh! Lemonade and crisps
And Windsor on the left
And four pretty girls
Conked-out in the lock.

"They might have a shear-pin.
Ahoy! 'Willow Talk'."
"Just look at that barge!"
"If you can hop off, chum,
I'll throw one down to you."
"I bet they're rich!"
"Here comes the rain again!"
"Who's got the cork?"

So, from the boat
And the river,
To the gate,
Remembering to shut it
After use.
Up gravelled side-road
To motorway again,
And finally, to bed
With a happy headache.

"Tie up for'ard!
Tie up aft!"
Work again tomorrow:
Then what, for a laugh . . . ?

Cathedral Beyond the Cornfield

Like dying applause,
The last thunderclaps rattle away behind the hills,
Leaving in their wake, the storm's residue,
An inky hue
Highlighting dark yellow waves
Tossed on a pale yellow sea,
A sea on which no engine throbs
Or silhouette bobs to jar the view
Until wind parts the corn
To show the spire...

A rocket to heaven which never takes off,
A slated conical hat beneath which the bishop is sat,
Haloed in his doorway by a gothic arch of light,
A tiny white bell, from a cut-out paper pattern,
Whilst above him, in the rain
His spire aspires in vain
To prick the scudding rain-clouds.

I shiver and drive away fast,
Glimpsing briefly in the mirror
A mast without a light
Becoming blunted by the night.

Death of the Rebel, Raddon

The 21st century 'Witch-Finder' General is home:
Having signed the Death Warrant
On a 52 month old Cocker
For daring to guard a bone.

His mistress came too near -
She meant no harm,
But he bit her arm,
This for the fourth time.

The vet proclaimed, "That's it! Sign."
Which I did, then felt sick,
For whose was the greatest crime,
The dog's or mine?

The Cuts

You cannot see the doctor
Nor can any of us:
He's examining the balls
On his abacus.

Garden Party

A flea sat down beneath the celery tree
And drank from the saucer of the old folks' tea.
Down flew a wasp and a bumble bee,
A storm fly, a pigeon and a capercaillie.

" 'Ello, 'ello. What's going on 'ere?"
Demanded a passing P.C.
"Are you the bee wot nicked the old folks' tea?
I think you better come along with me!"

"You leave him alone!"
Said the bee's big brother, Buzzer.
"Me and Wally Wasp might sting you... see!"
The storm fly joined in, excitedly:

"Look what's left - a big cream cake.
Some of that I'll certainly take!
Me, oh my! I'm such a lucky fly.
Look what else is left...
A big, pork pie!"

Growing Pains

London 1960's

To the single, rented room
Of the greedy gas meter,
Of the candlewick bedspread
And the cistern in the night,
Come the optimistic young
To live abreast of persons topical,
As though from mere proximity
To win a similar right.

And what if they succeed
Amongst the fashionable or latest?
At best all they can hope to be
Is third or second greatest.
More unique, are they who search
For self-originality,
If only that the heart is searched…
Not the heart's locality

Ha, Ha, Ha !

A man I knew
Bought a thirty-foot yacht,
Insured his wife,
Then pushed her off.
'Ha, ha, ha !'

He giggled and trembled
And tried to take stock.
He went down below
And took a tot,
Then another and another.

The thirty-foot yacht
Smashed into a rock.
Sadly for him,
But luckily for me,
She could swim
But he could not.

'Ha, ha, ha !'

"Look away, Fred, Look away!"

" 'Ello, boys! Not dancin'?
My name's Maureen
An' this is my friend, Kate.
We makes Swiss rolls
Down at the tradin' estate.
The money comes in 'andy
But the job 'aint up to much:
She puts the jam in
An' I rolls 'em up!

'Ere, ' ang on, fellers! Where yuh goin' ?"

The Bank Manager's Statement

"Sorry, Dad!
I've blown my savings
On a motor bike;
I'm off to see the World.
Cheerio!"

"Now just a minute, lad!
You come back here!
There's more to money
Than just *life*,
You know!

Head in the Clouds

Where do we go at the end of the show?
Religious faiths claim to know where's best.
But I suggest the sky -
Is as good a place as any, to finally rest.

Sat in garden or park,
What do we see, looking up?
Shapes of animals, of you and me,
Lying horizontally, embodied in cumulus.

Mouths open, heads covered by nets of cauliflower florets,
Wind changes the shapes from human to animal and vice-versa.
The compost of us heats and heat rises. Is that how we get there?
Condensation or divine ascension? We'll never know.

Only that sky is earth's blotting paper,
Eternity's slide-show in the clouds,
Showing us on the ground
Where closure may be found.

Old Jazzers

They wear beards, bandanas,
Fishermen's smocks,
Fagged-out chukka boots
And flame-red socks,
Corduroy trousers
And sheepskin tops
And they loiter in the doorways
Of bric-a-brac shops.

They are the 'Jazzers!'
The old Jazzers!

They're in Norfolk,
Oxford, Richmond, Putney,
Or 'letchering' in Art
At a local University
To slim, stunning girls
With Minis and money,
Who come up from Hampshire
In defiance of Mummy.

Bloody 'Jazzers!'
Jazzers and their 'molls!'

Others abound
Above harbours in Cornwall;
In north-facing studios
Bashing up marble -
Or another man's wife –
Twice-weekly contrite
To encourage a bruise
From his palette-knife handle.

Watch out, ladies!
A 'Jazzer' will 'ave yer!

They puff bendy pipes,
Know where aubergines are sold;
But - though sixty and furry –
Cannot *possibly* be old,
Because their self-appointed daughters -
Those attentive molls -
Replace steam in their kettles
And cream in their rolls.

Good little girls
Do what they are told!

Their habitat is Hampstead
Or on barges down at Kew;
Their plumage, studied scruffiness;
Their song, a book-review.
Their breeding is prolific,
Yet school-fees very few . . .
God knows how they do it
But they do!

Bloated,
Salt and pepper bearded *BADGERS* !

Still . . .
It wouldn't go amiss
If - when I'm pushing sixty -
A girl on *my* barge
Shrugged off her bikini
And struck a leggy pose
To taunt a young man on a bridge,
Softly swearing to himself
As this morning, I did,
Looking down upon a 'Jazzer'
A lucky, razmatazzer and his 'moll.'

The Deeply Felt

A good poem is like the middle of a swimming pool;
Not too deep or too shallow;
Not too wide or too narrow.

 A good poem is a tiny star
Seen through a door, left ajar
Drawing us in to the deeply felt

A good poem is neither too cryptic nor too mystic:
Just a teased-out truth which everyone knows,
But only a poem really shows.

Raddon Top

We've picked the place it will finally be,
Not down among the gravestones' stony tongues
But up on the ridge-line of Raddon Top,
Against the base of a windswept tree -
Adding our ashes to those of our dog.

We don't mind; the wife and me,
If occasionally,
Dogs, sheep, foxes, rabbits and ramblers
Add their pee to the scenery,
Before grazing, trotting, hopping
And walking past the dust of us.

Quentin & Bert, September 1940

Quentin was an officer,
And Bert? Bert was his 'erk',
Keeping Spitfire, shoes, and Quentin's blues
'Spiffed-up' and free from dirt.

Quentin had the background
So, in keeping with the game,
Bert put the petrol in
And Quentin flew the plane.

Bert filled up the Spit' at four
And Quentin's cup at five,
Then Quentin 'went-in' over Deal.
And Bert? Well, Bert survived!

Tug O'War

Heave-ho!
Tug o'war
Sunny hill versus rainswept moor,
Mild against the raw.

Spring is on its feet,
Winter's on the floor.
Heave-ho!
Tug o'war.

It's the seasonal see-saw;
Come back in October
And we'll show you more.
Heave-ho! Tug o'war.

Return Ticket

Indifferent, anonymous blackness
Randomly punctured
By pin-pricks of light,
Lasering through the crust,
Heralding . . . *life*.
Six pounds of kicking, piddling,
Dribbling sibling or first-born,
Leaving a halo of spittle
From its gripple on a nipple.
Thus emerges yet another front-loaded
Pink, black, brown or yellow one;
Bouncing down the chute
Onto the 'goods-outward' tray.

Not far away,
Hemmed-in by bus-routes, stone walls
And Leylandii,
Among the gaps in the crumbling, stony, dentures,
A freshly-dug mound
Marks a hole in the ground
In urgent need of a filling.
It is from such discreet compost heaps
On the margins of towns
That the 'perishables,' now past their 'live-by' dates,
Are mumbled away on their return-journeys.
The term'return' on one's metaphysical ticket
Entitles the holder to travel
From temporary white
Back into permanent, eternal black.
So know this inescapable fact . . .
You'll need more than just a packed-lunch !

"We're Closing Down Now…"

He died as he lived;
In front of the telly
Four cans and a slipper
On the floor;
Chicken leg on belly;
Mouth still open
From the last snore.

Had he survived
Just one day more,
Would he have whined,
" 'Snot my fault;
I 'ad it rough."

No…
Because for him,
How he lived
Was enough.

Yum! Yum!

The lion ambled away
Licking his lips;
One *very* satisfied cat.
Leaving behind
The missionary's crumpled hat
And the dedication
Inscribed within:

'To the very Rev.Grundy.
From the Methodists of Lundy.
May God be with you in Africa,
Taming the godless
And feeding the hungry.'

Winter

Geese glide in from the Arctic to the U.K.
Swallows fly the other way, to Africa.

Days shorten; skies darken; ice attacks pipes, not lagged,
Forging spears from outside taps.

Whiskers of frost drape lawns and leaves;
Mercury drops; butter hardens; asthmatics wheeze.

Drawers are ransacked for fleecy tops,
Hats, scarves, gloves and socks.

Cordials, ice-creams and salads make way
For soups, stews, hotpots, curries and cocoa.

Boilers are serviced; logs delivered; shovels retrieved;
Chimneys swept and gutters cleared.

Backlit branches, a witch's broom,
Brush away clouds from the face of the moon.

And us? We succumb...
Retreating under covers until Spring returns the sun.

Made in the USA
Charleston, SC
02 May 2014